I0416633

This book is dedicated to people who love cute rabbits.

TIAGO PIXEL
2024

This Book Belongs to:

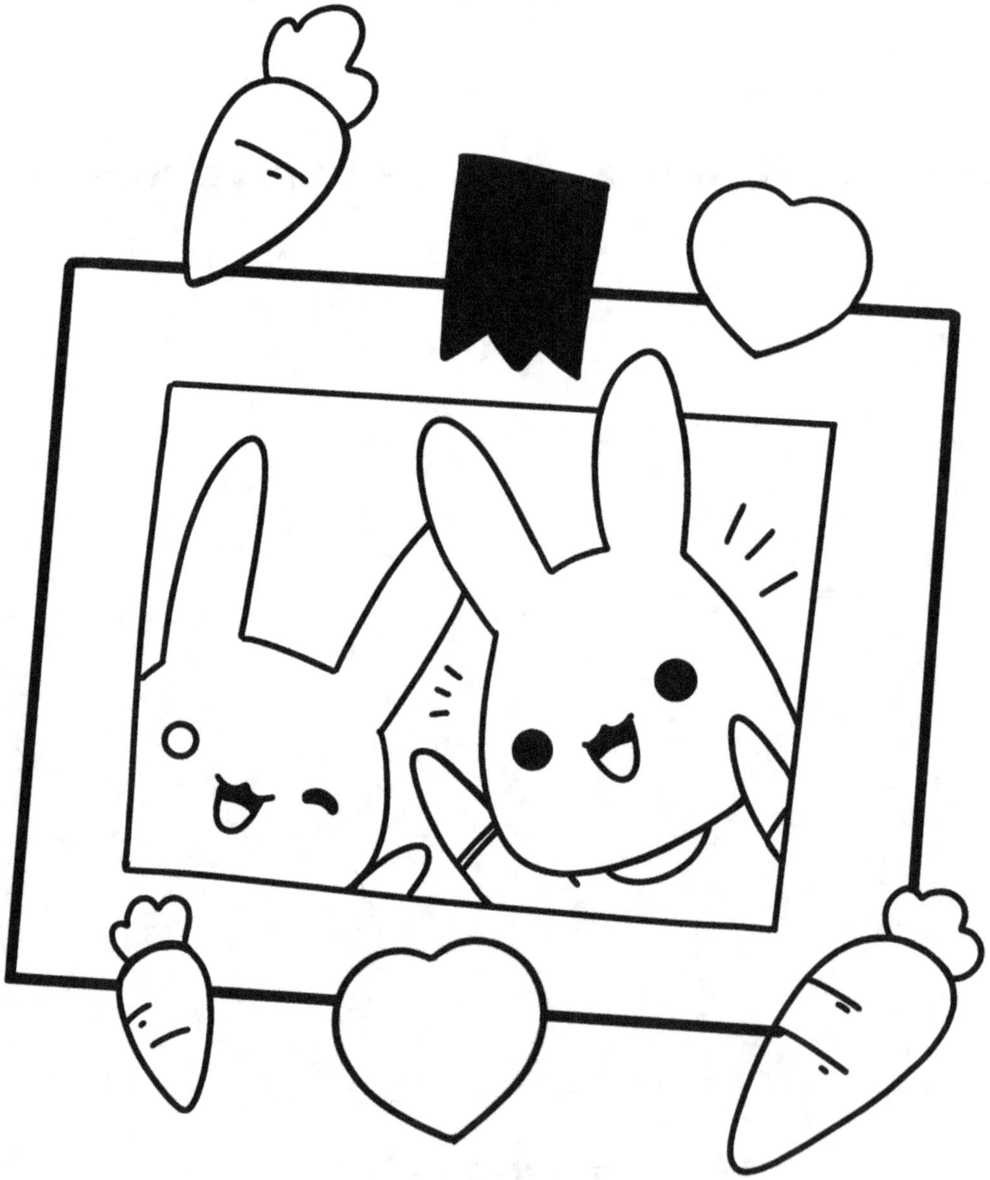

TIAGO PIXEL publications ©

Test Color Page

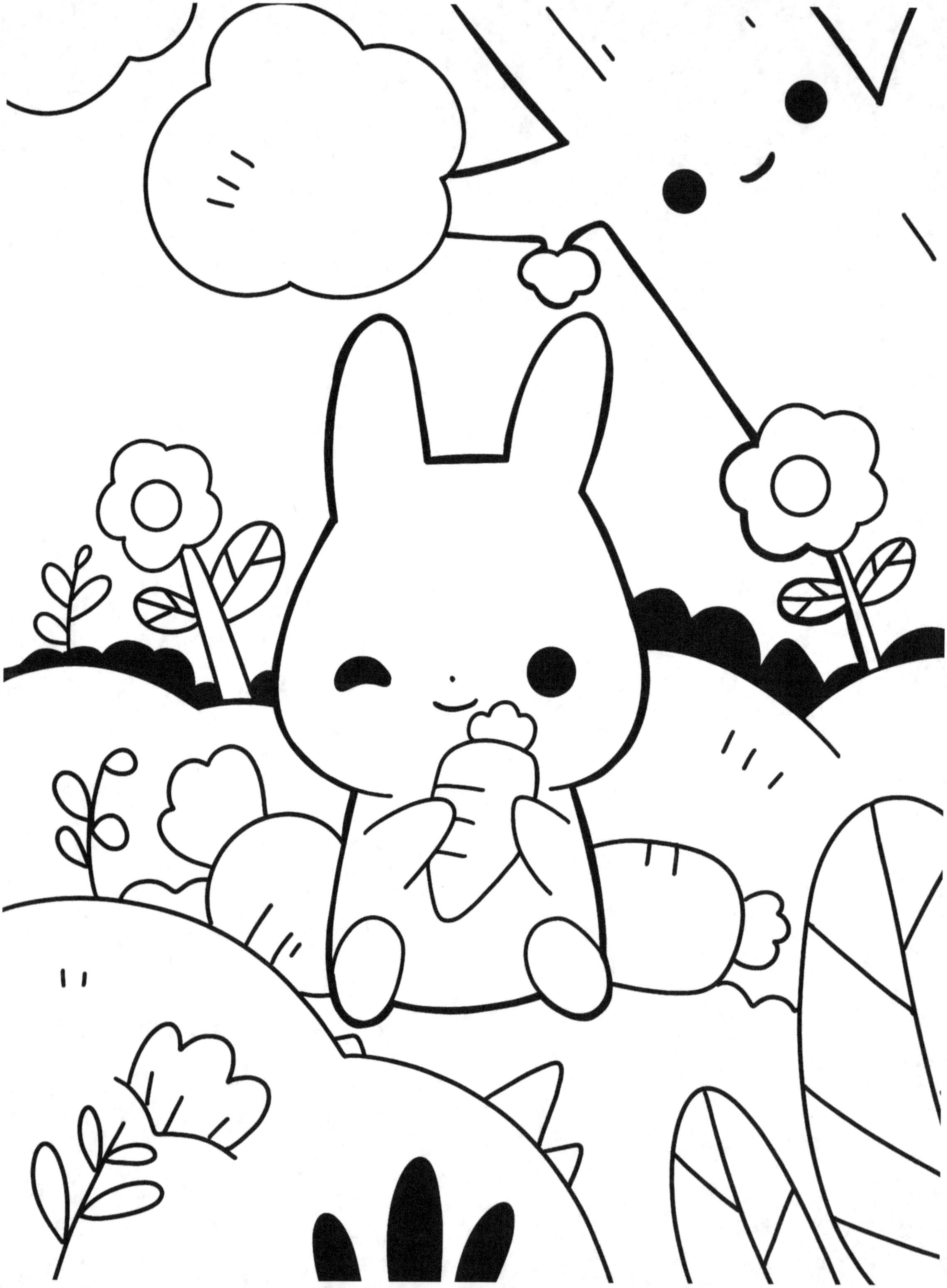

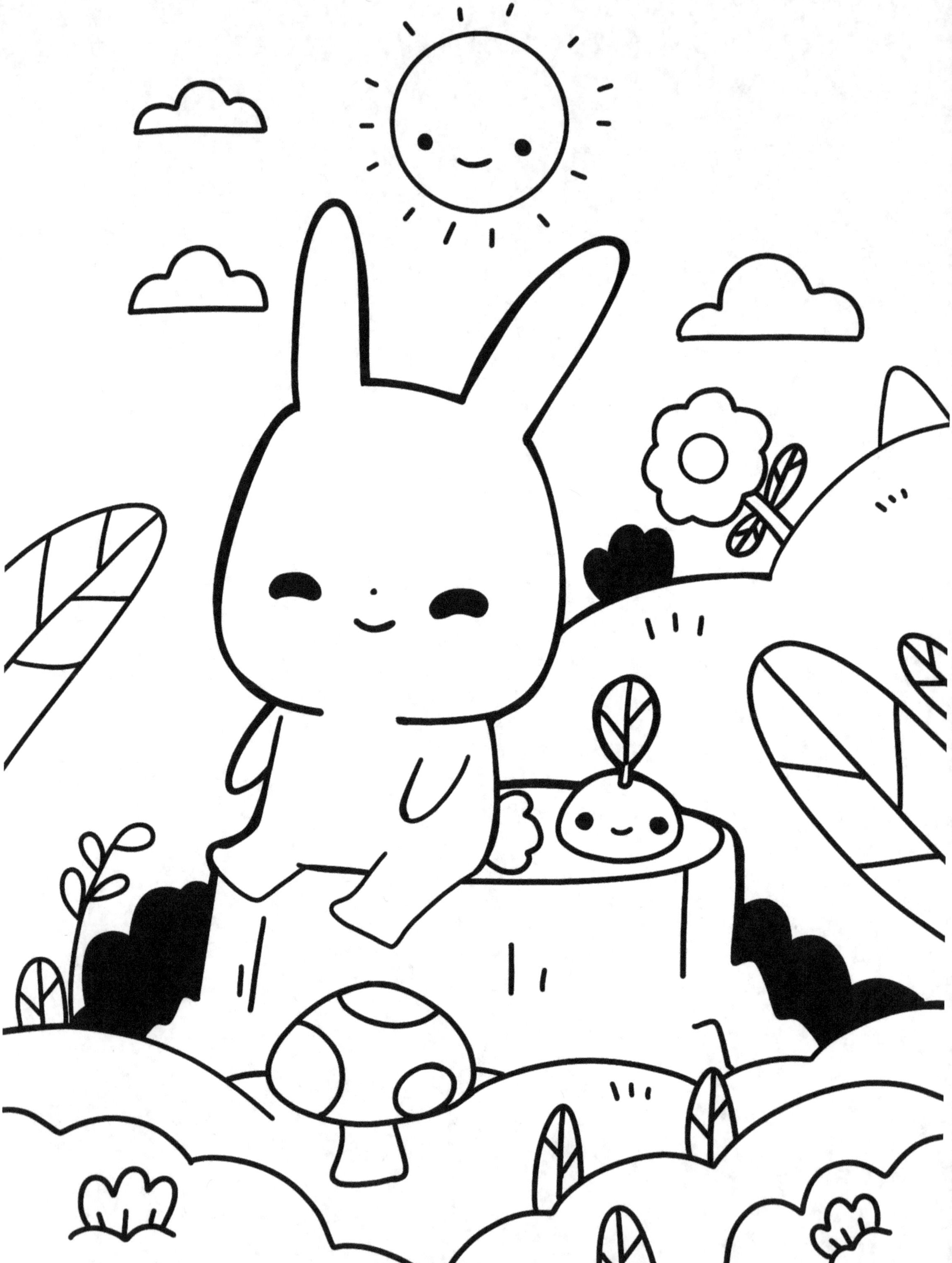

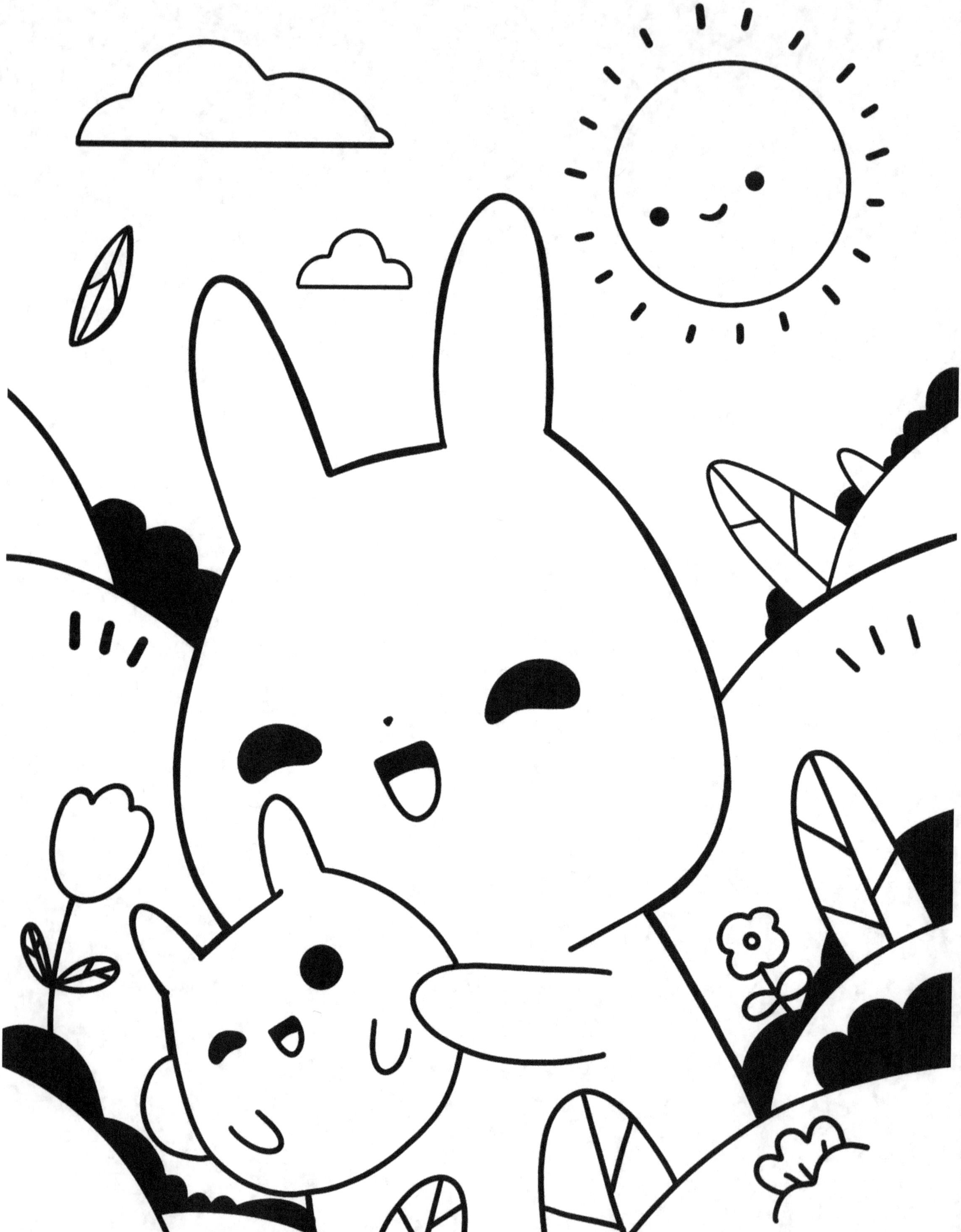

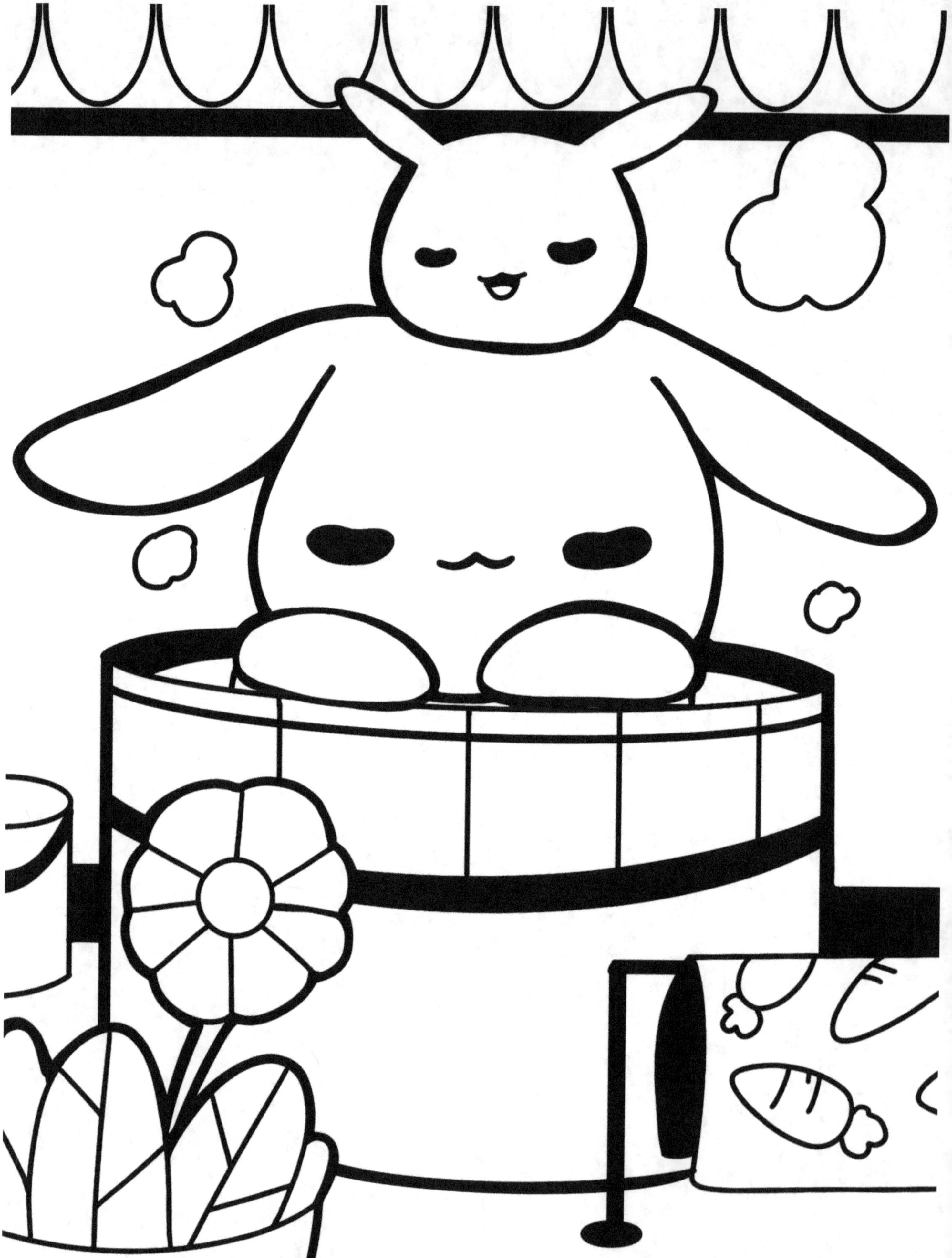

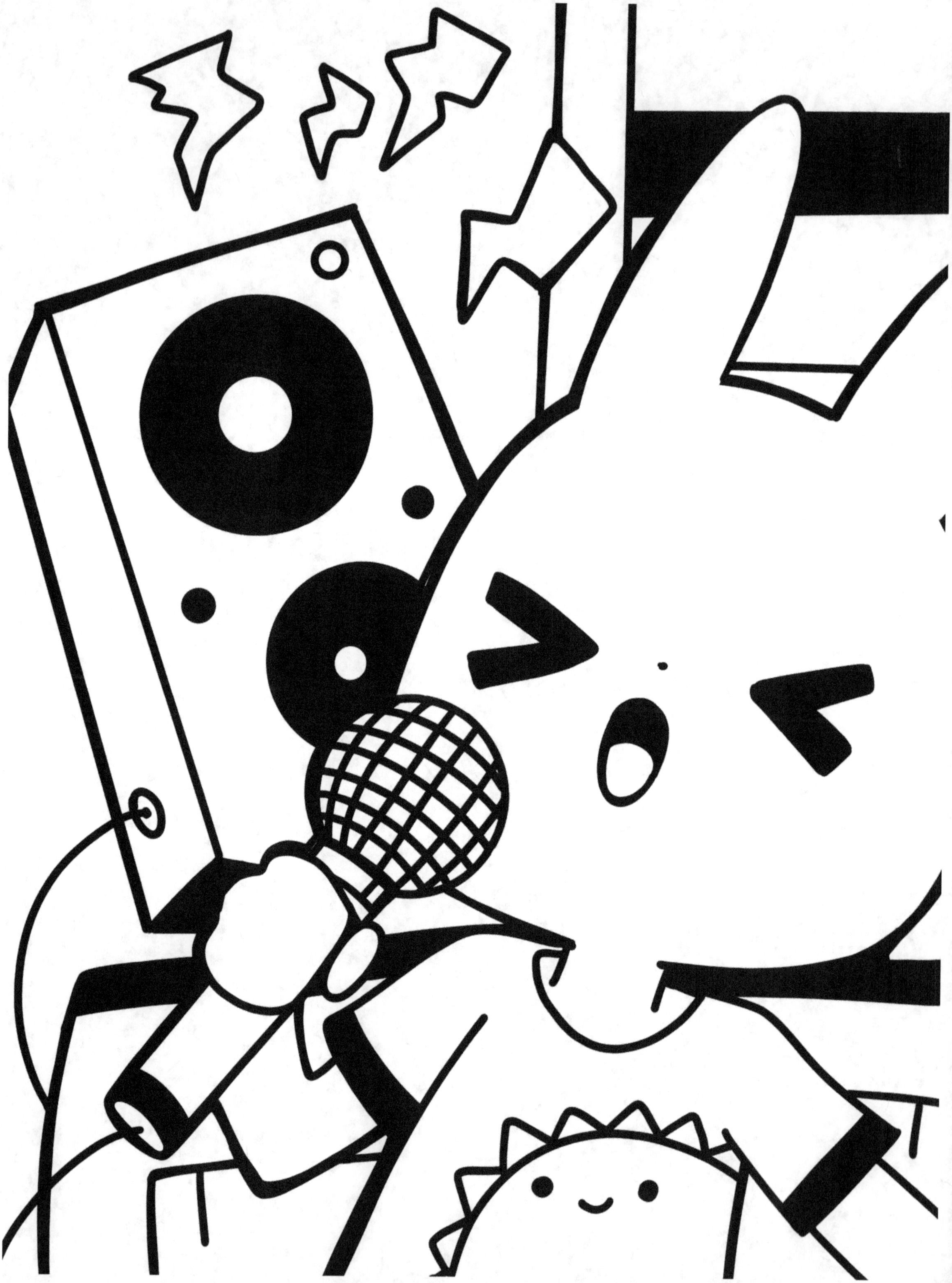

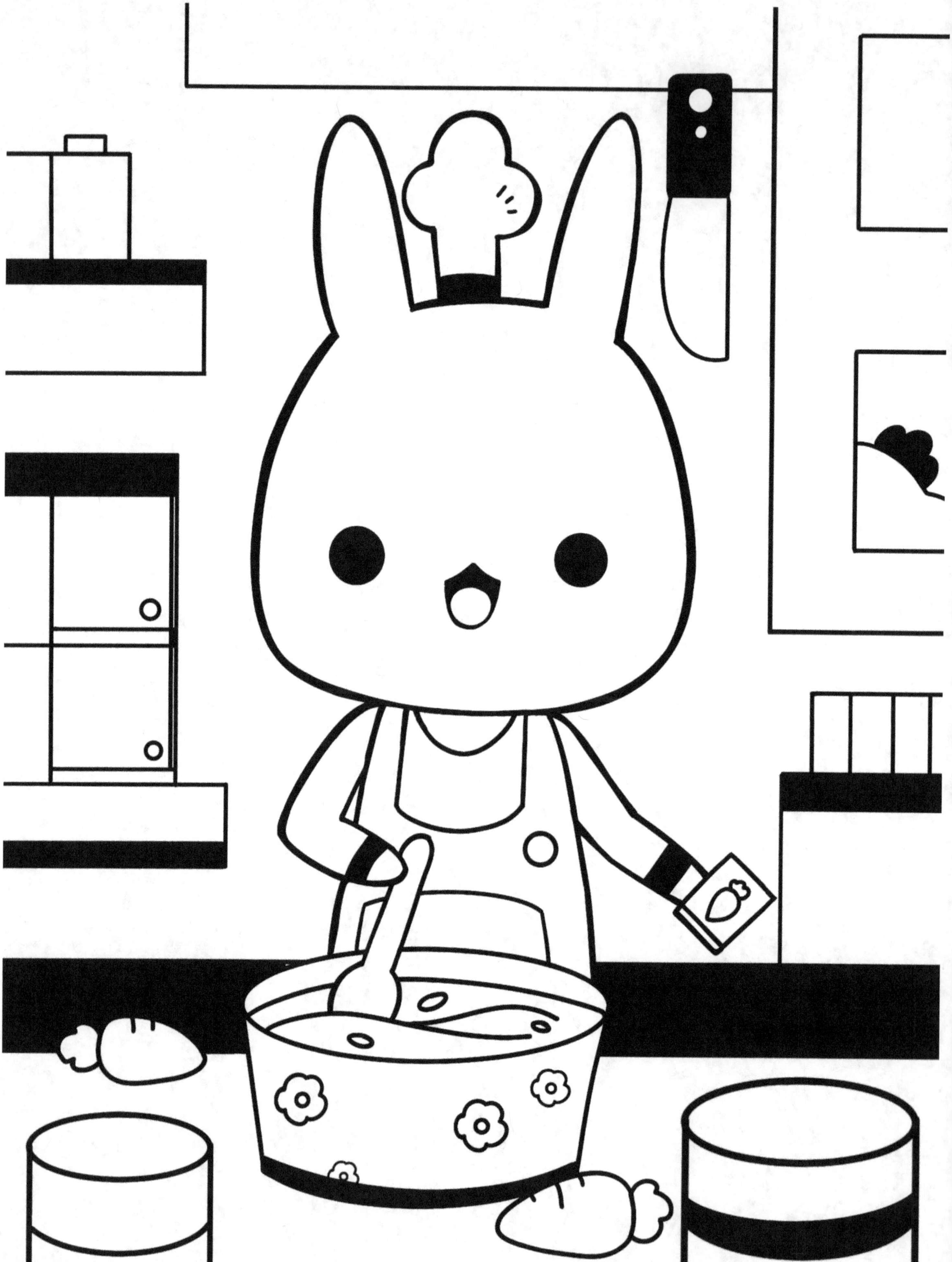

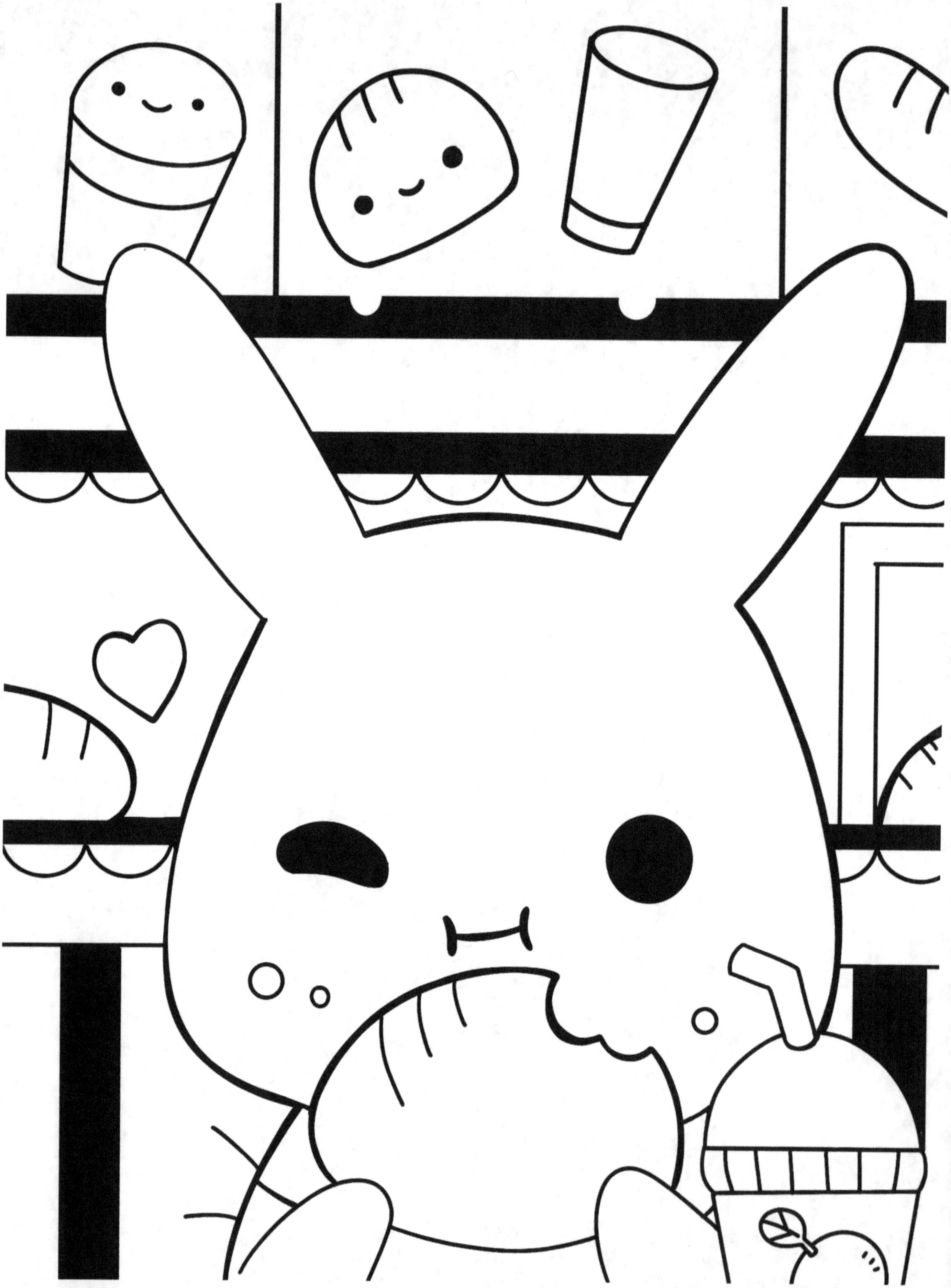

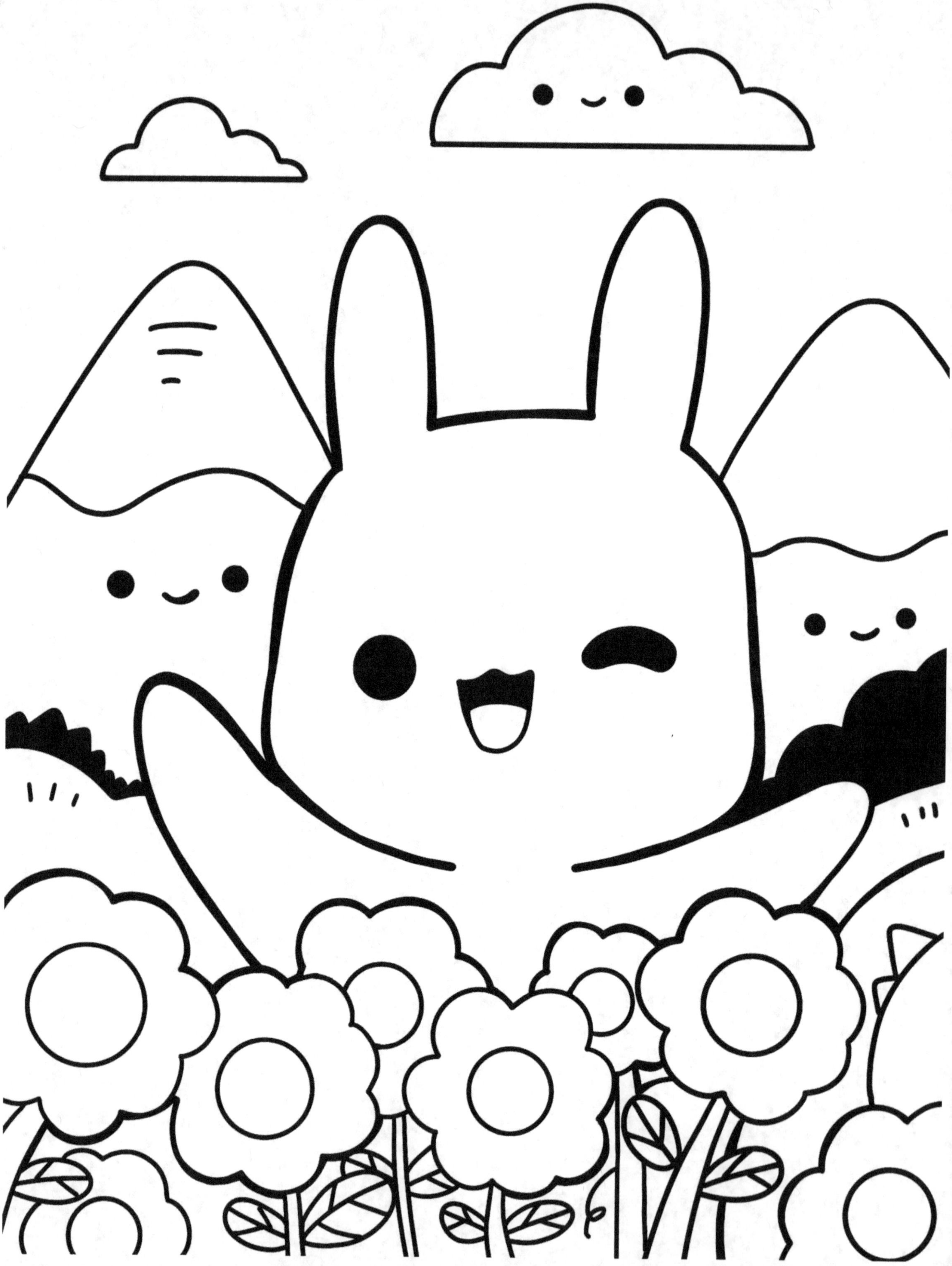

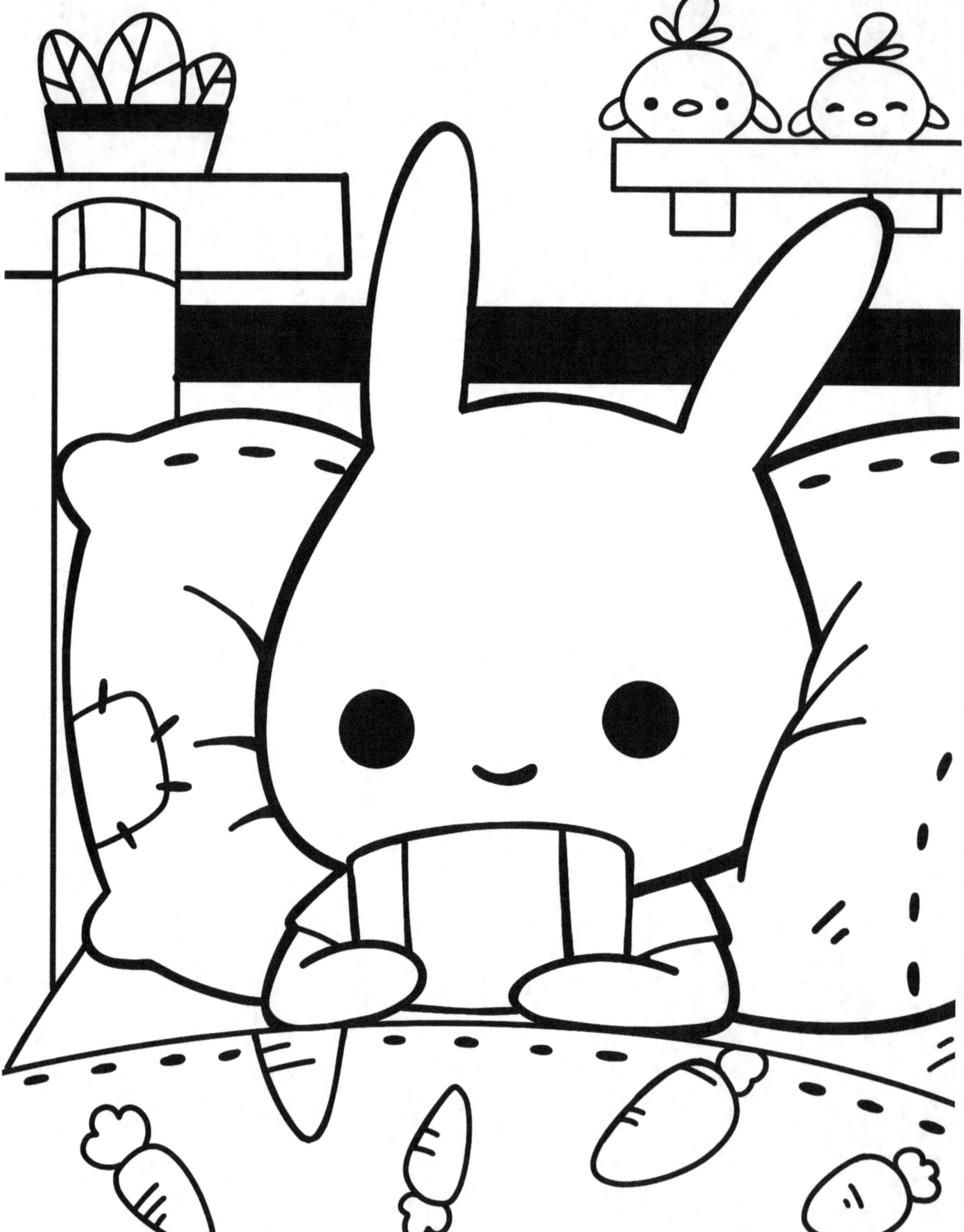

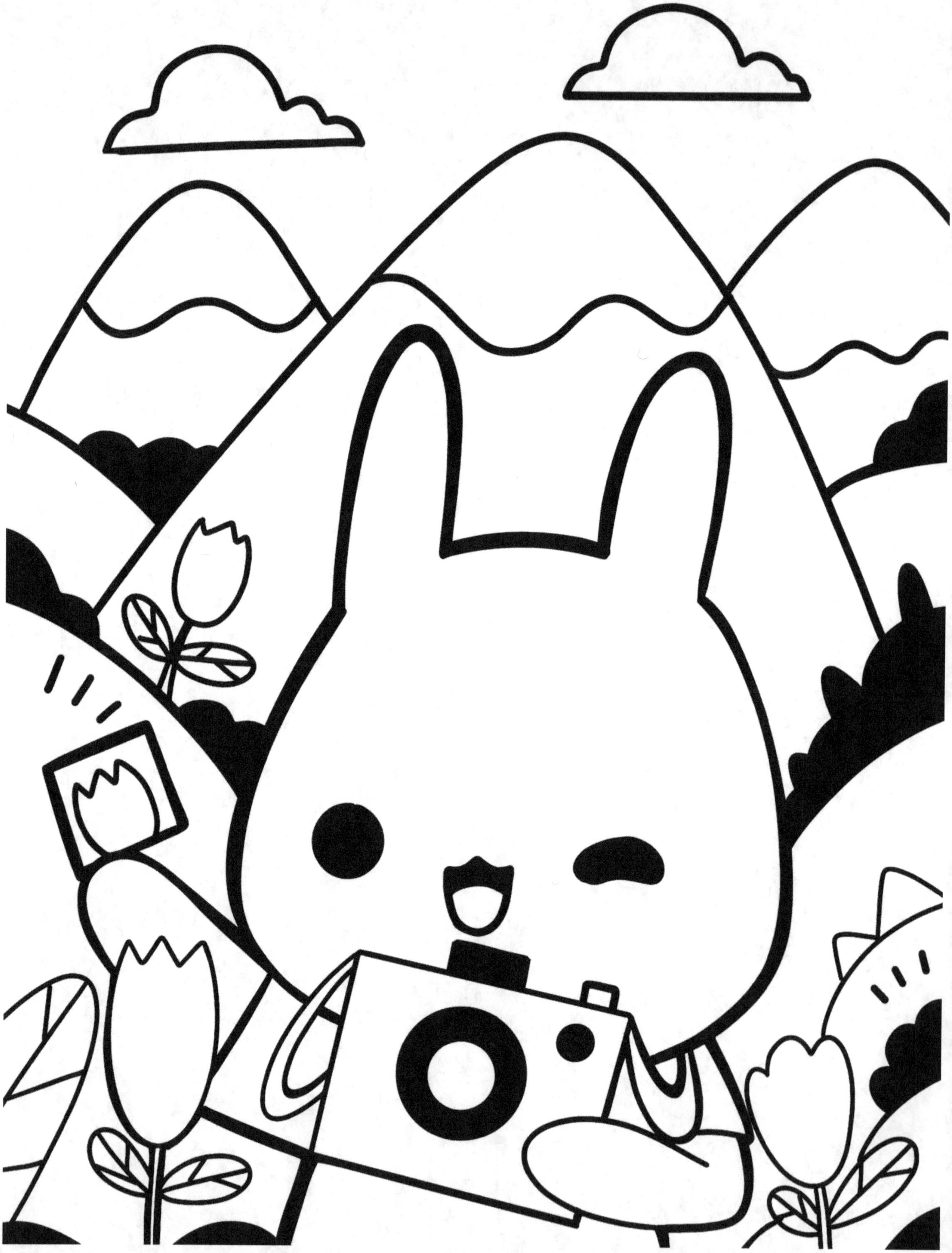

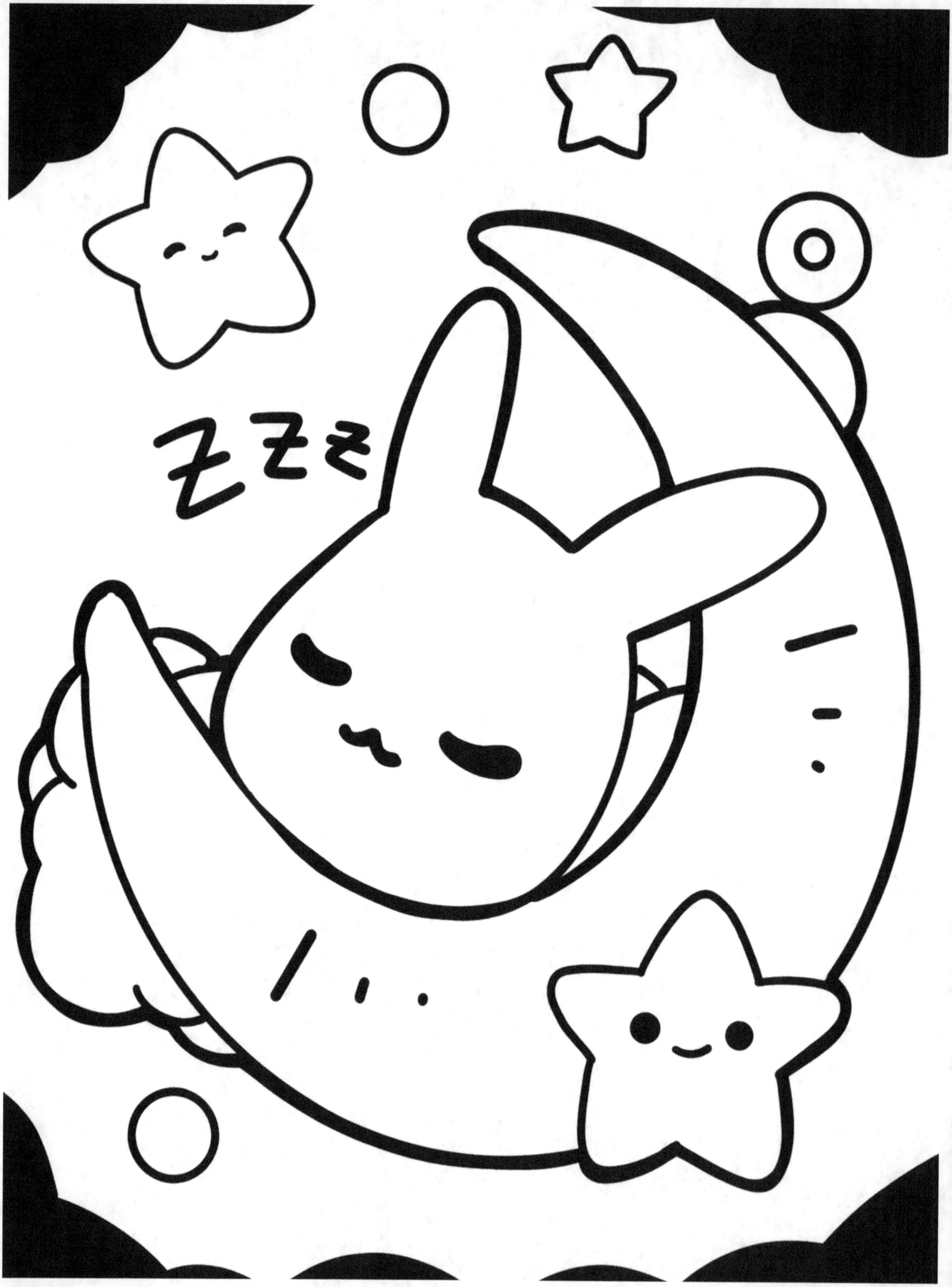
Zzz

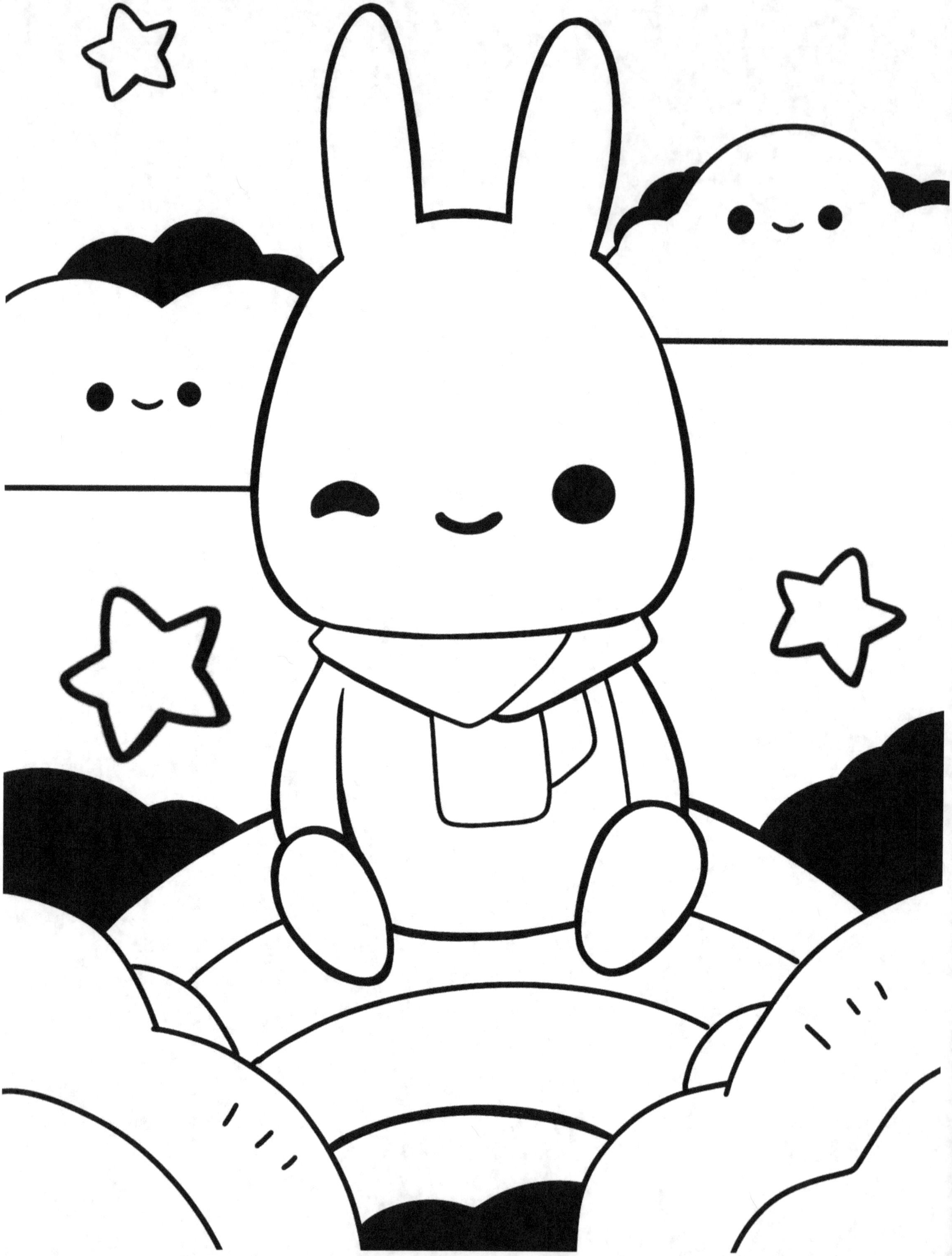

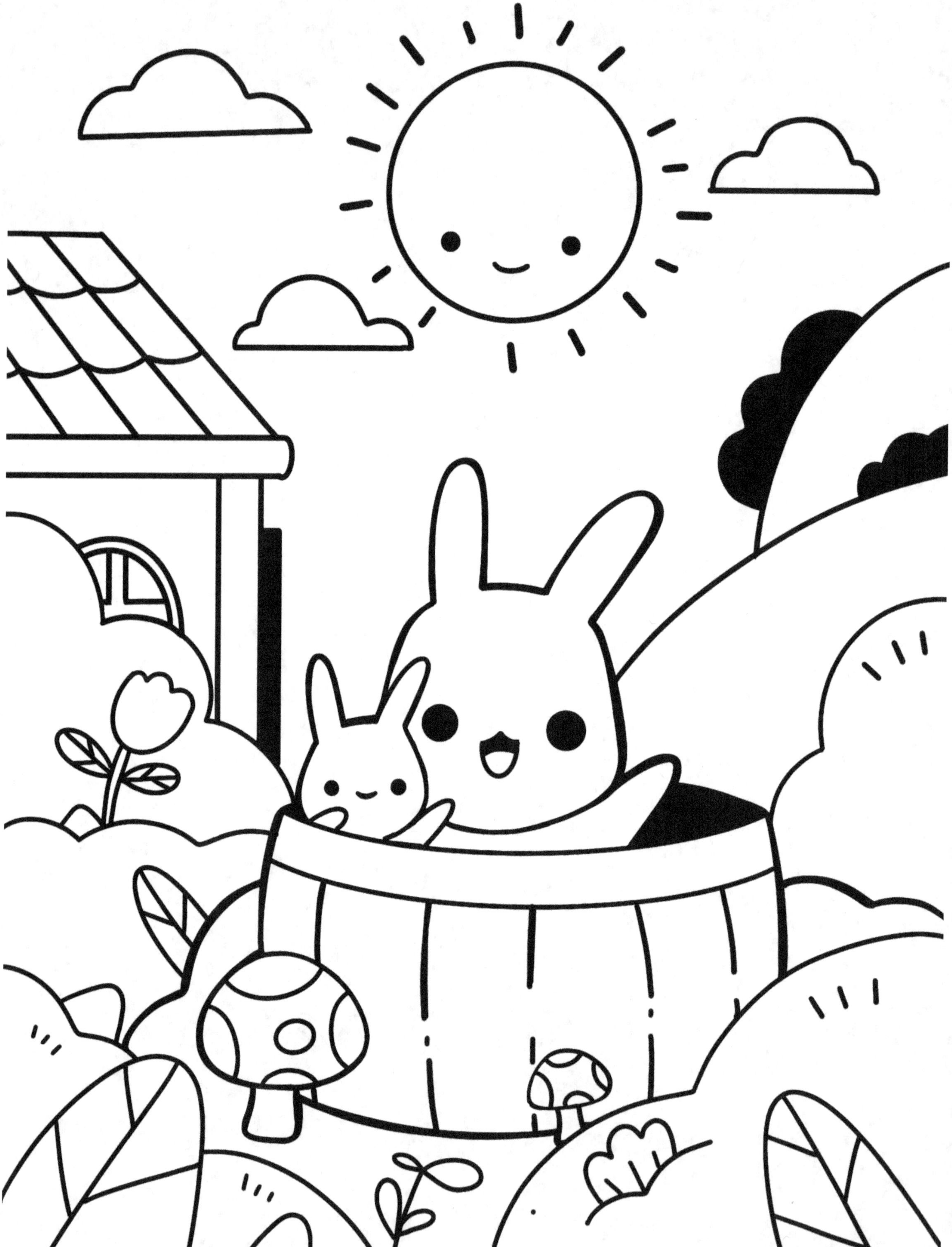

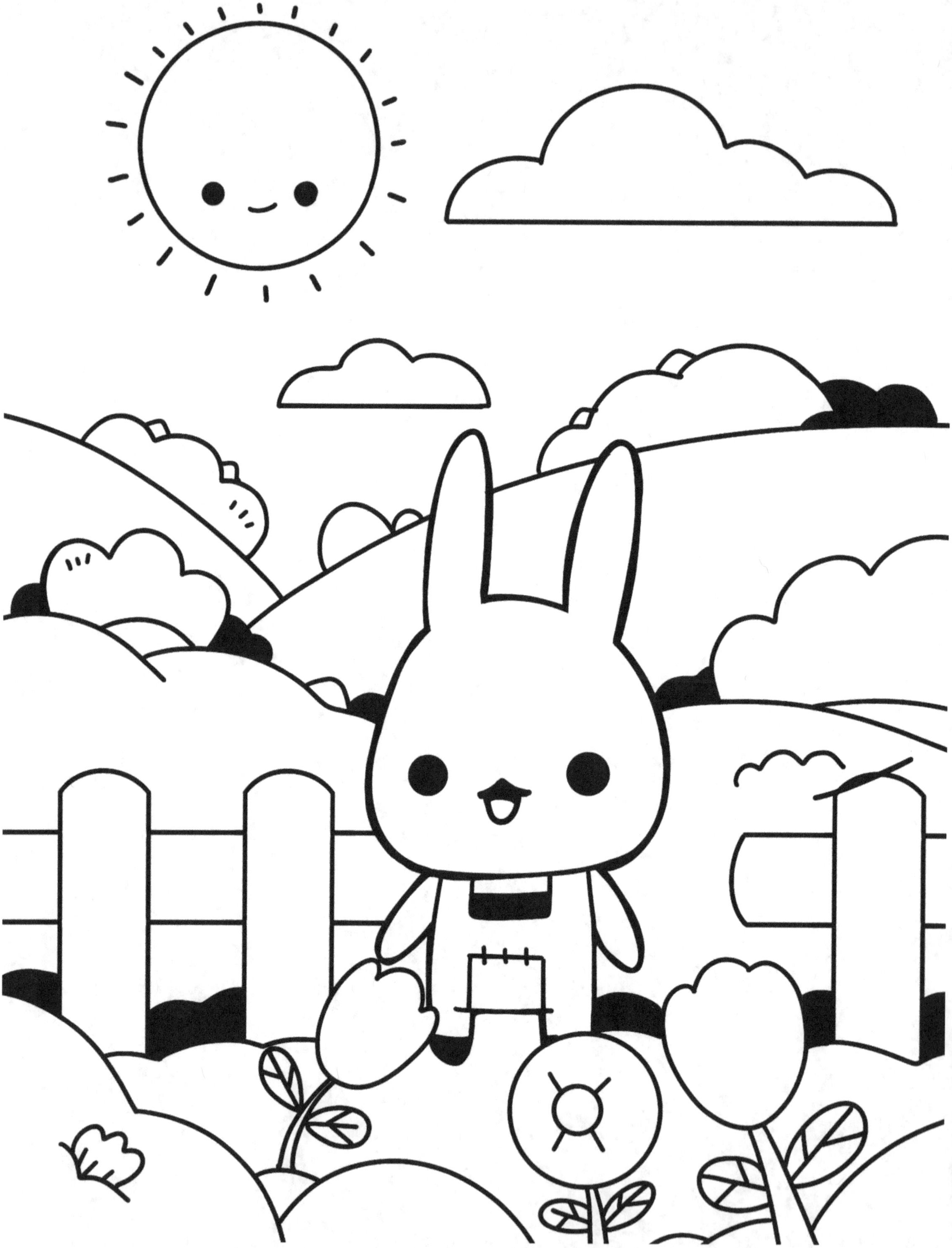

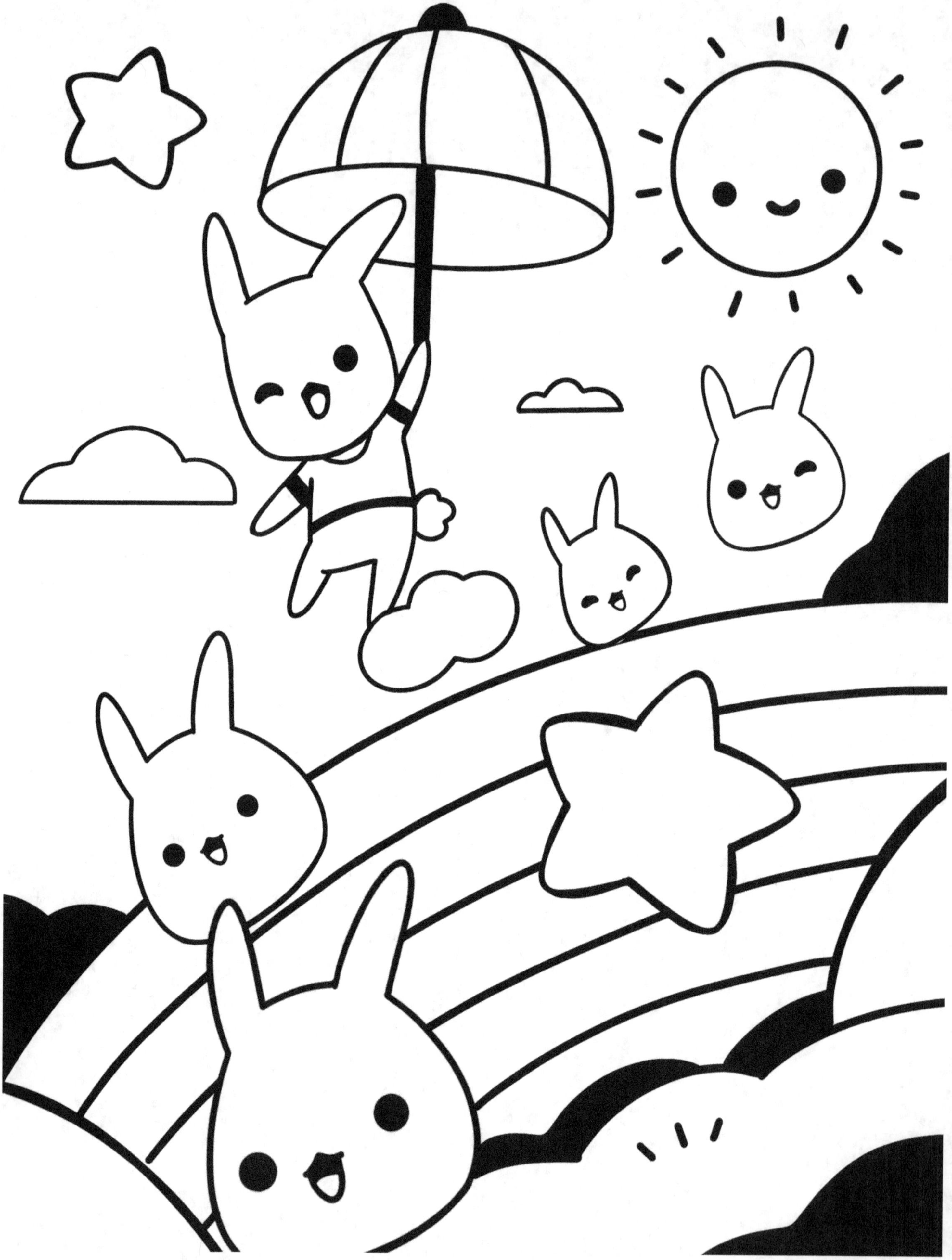

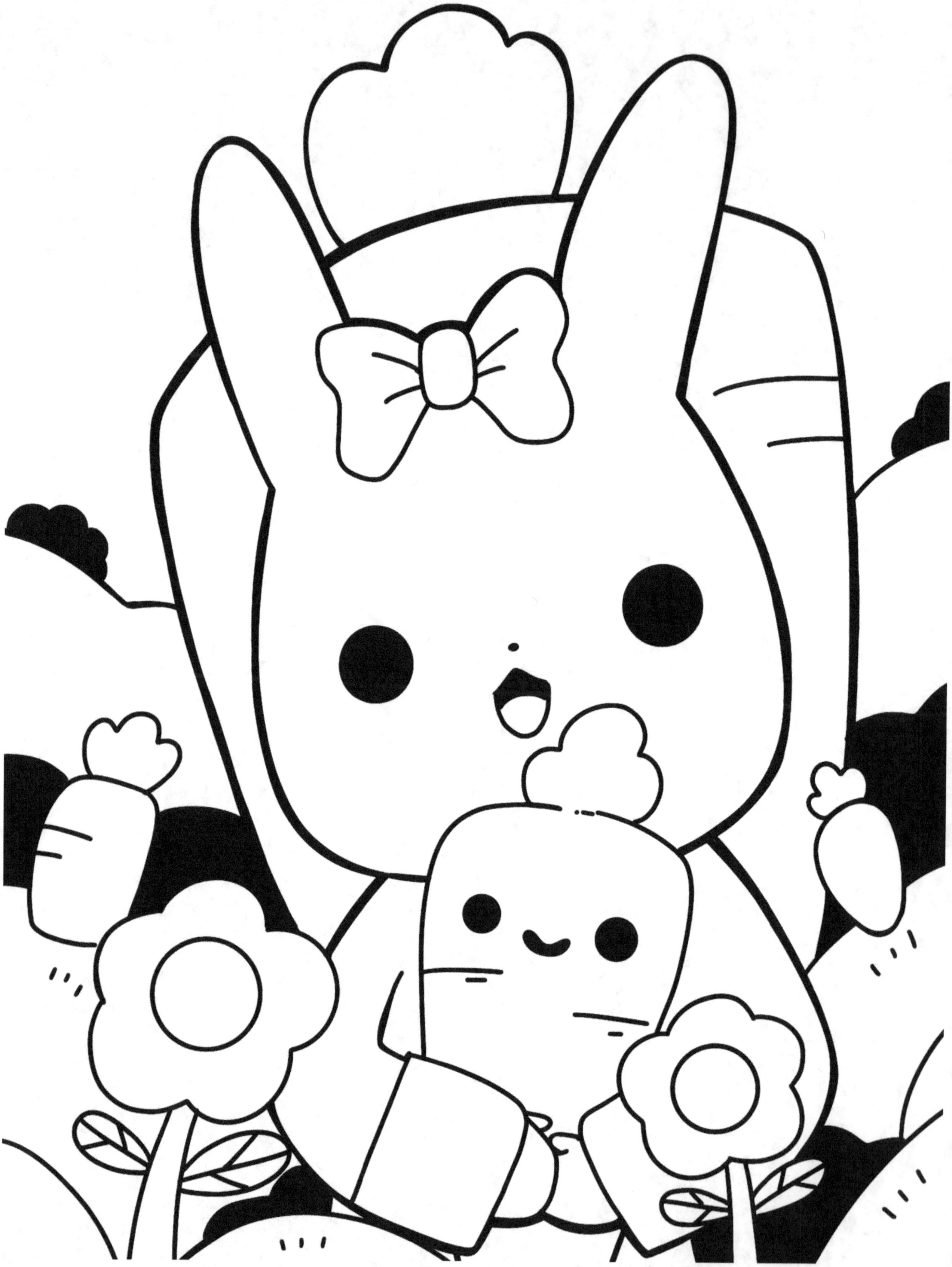

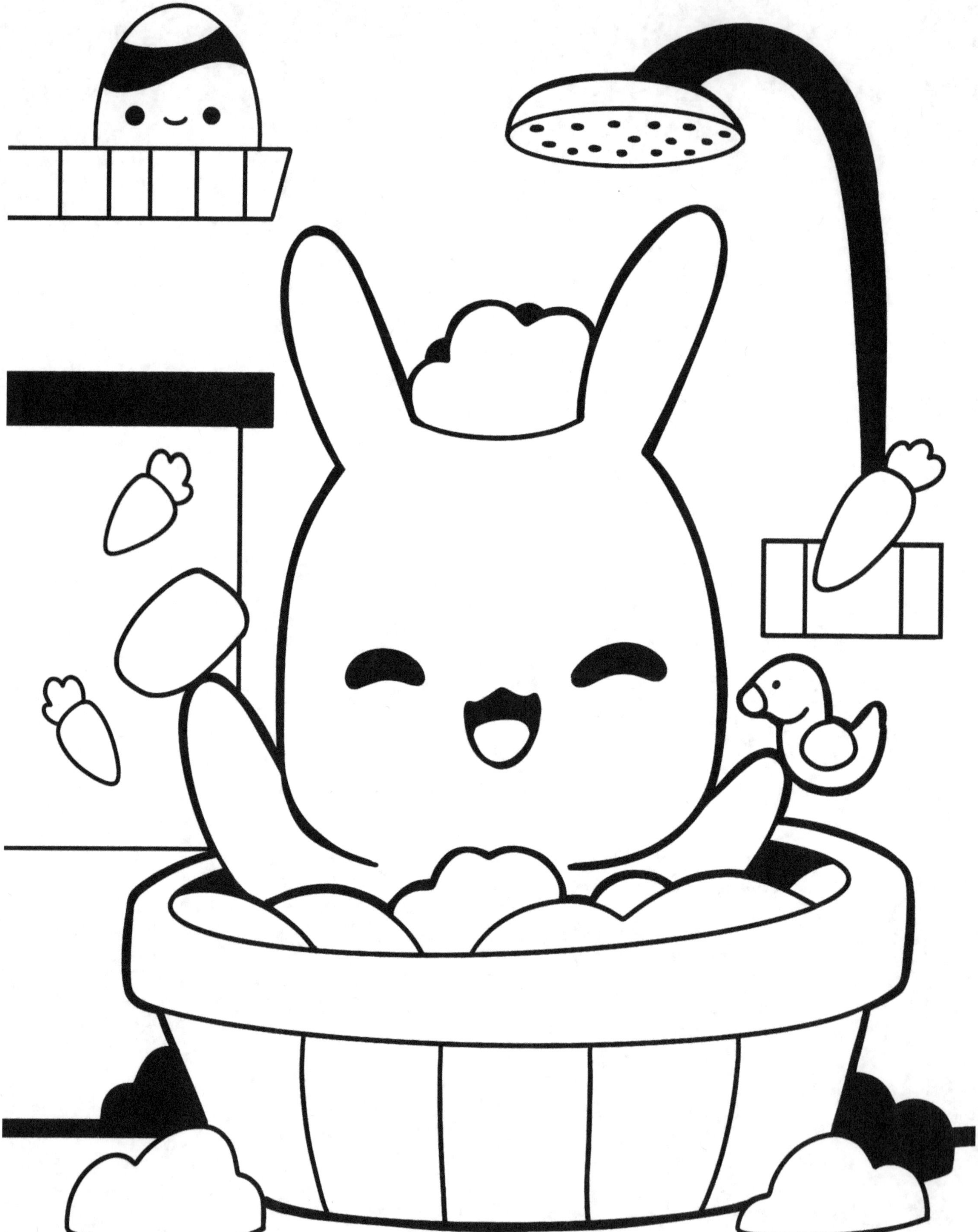

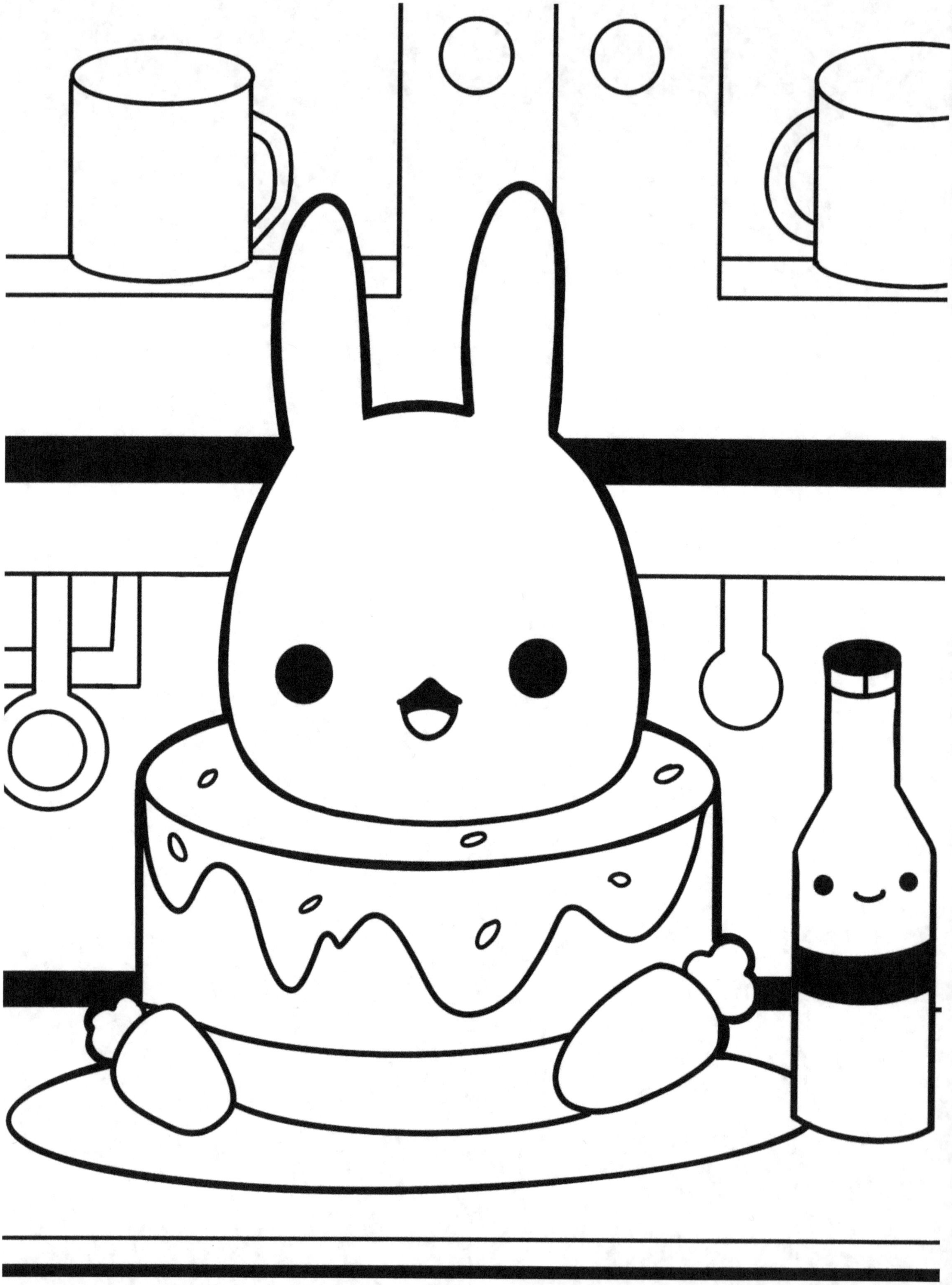

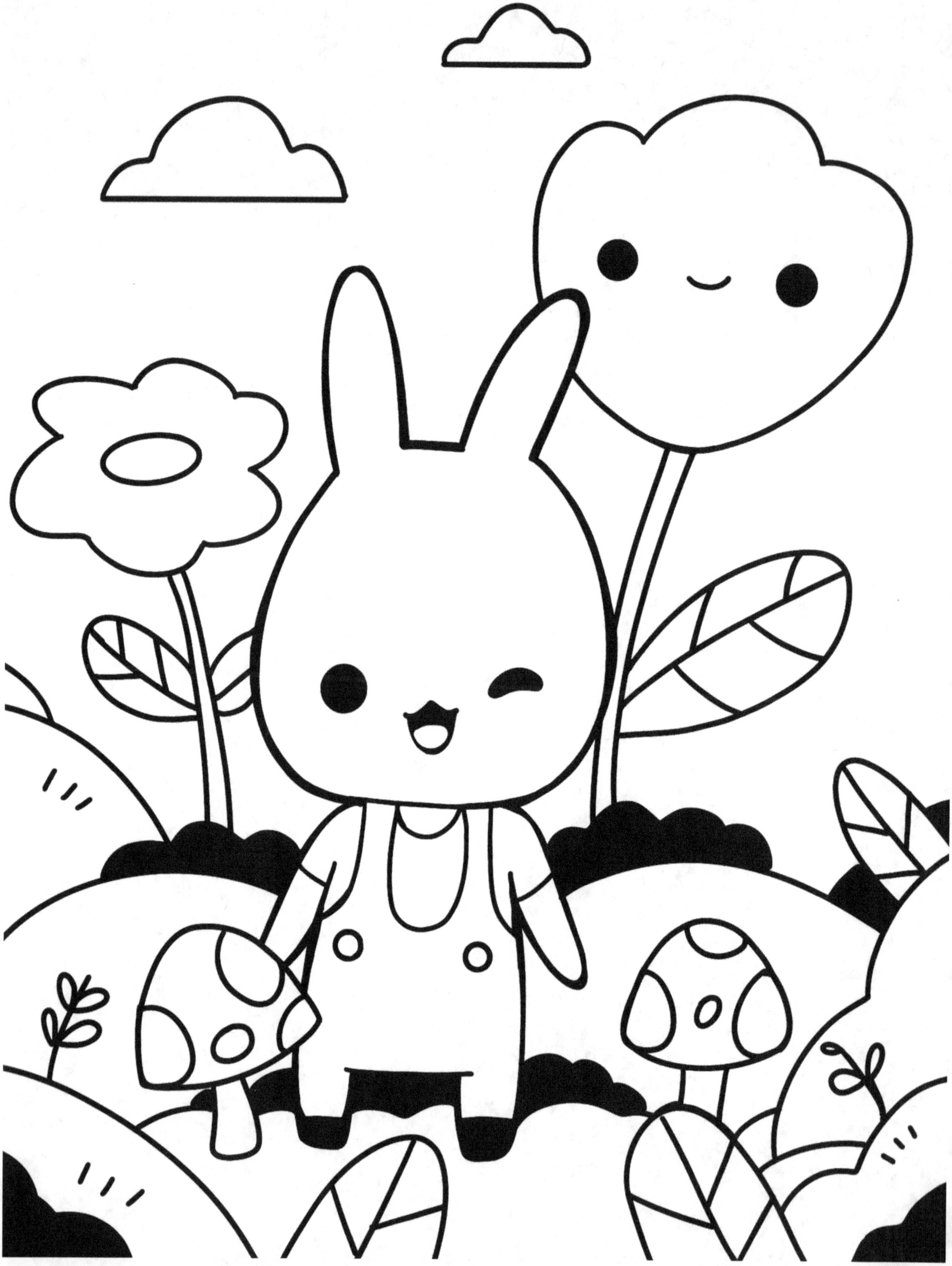

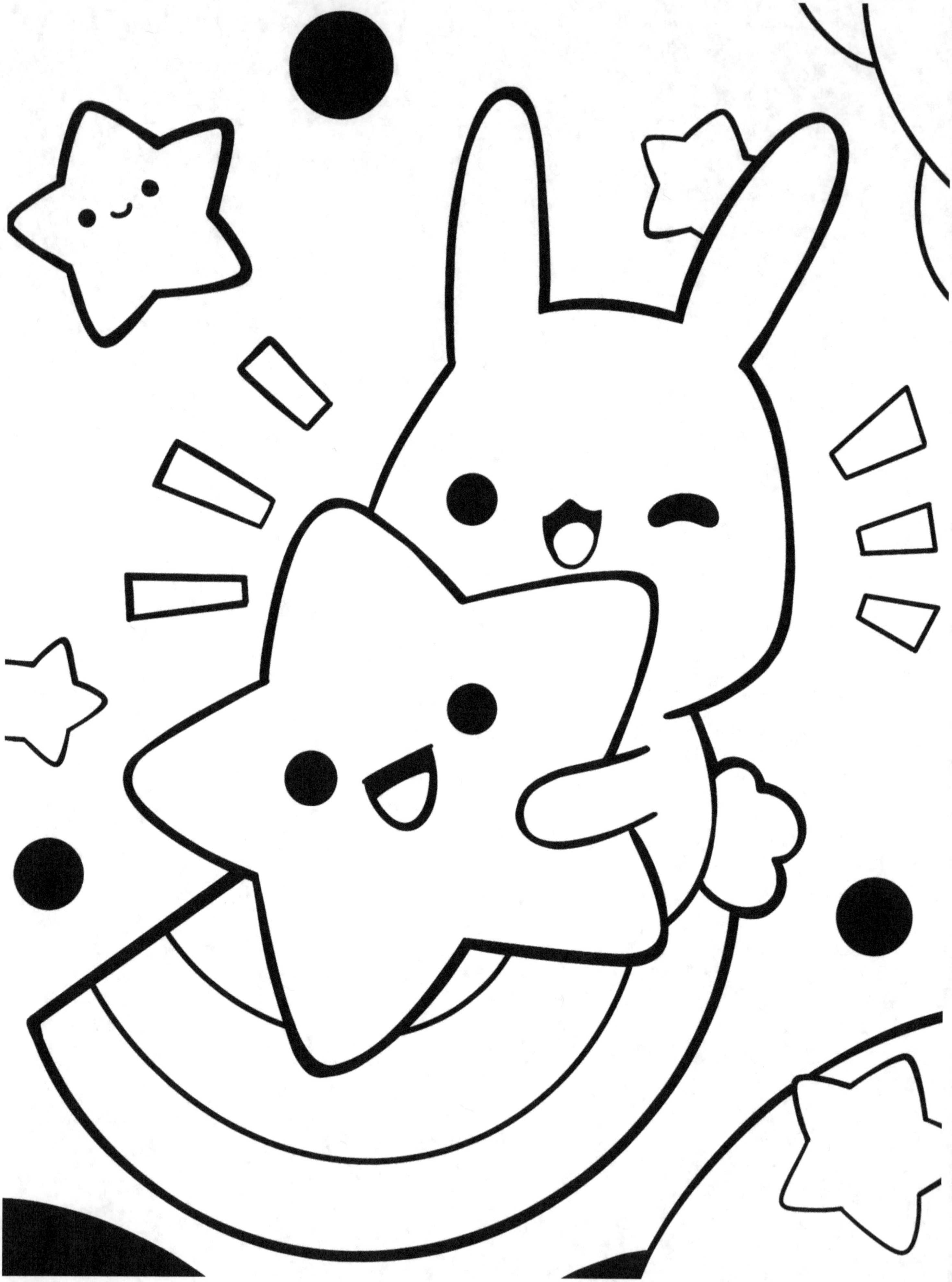

www.ingramcontent.com/pod-product-compliance
Lightning Source LLC
Chambersburg PA
CBHW081003290526
45795CB00009B/3063